RISK ASSESSMENT

TABLE OF CONTENTS

CHAPTER 1

INTRODUCTION TO RISK ASSESSMENT

1.1 DEFINITION OF RISK ASSESSMENT

Risk assessment is a systematic and structured process of evaluating potential risks, or the likelihood and impact of events that could negatively affect an organization or project. The purpose of risk assessment is to understand and prioritize risks, to determine the most appropriate risk management strategies, and to improve decision-making in the face of uncertainty.

1.2 SIGNIFICANCE OF RISK ASSESSMENT

Risk assessment is crucial for organizations of all sizes and across all industries, as it helps to ensure that resources are allocated effectively, goals are achieved, and negative impacts are minimized. By identifying and assessing risks, organizations can make informed decisions, allocate resources more effectively, and be better prepared to respond to unexpected events.

1.3 OVERVIEW OF THE RISK ASSESSMENT PROCESS

The risk assessment process typically involves four key steps:

- Identification of risks

- Analysis of risks

- Mitigation of risks

- Management of risks

In the identification stage, risks are identified through a variety of methods, such as brainstorming, SWOT analysis, and scenario analysis. In the analysis stage, risks are evaluated based on their likelihood and potential impact. In the mitigation stage, strategies are developed to reduce the likelihood and impact of risks, such as mitigation, transfer, and avoidance. Finally, in the management stage, the risk management plan is implemented, and risks are monitored and reviewed regularly to ensure that they are being effectively managed.

1.4 KEY ELEMENTS OF EFFECTIVE RISK ASSESSMENT

Effective risk assessment requires a systematic and structured approach, and a thorough understanding of the organization or project being assessed. It also requires clear communication, collaboration, and a commitment to continuous improvement.

Other key elements of effective risk assessment include:

- Clear identification of risks
- Comprehensive analysis of risks
- Appropriate risk mitigation strategies
- Effective risk management processes
- Regular monitoring and review of risks

1.5 PURPOSE AND SCOPE OF THE BOOK

The purpose of this book is to provide a comprehensive and practical guide to risk assessment. It covers the key principles and best practices of risk assessment, and provides a thorough understanding of the risk assessment process, including identification, analysis, mitigation, and management. The book is intended for professionals in risk management, as well as students, researchers, and anyone interested in understanding the process of risk assessment.

1.6 OVERVIEW OF THE REMAINING CHAPTERS

The book is organized into 10 chapters, each focusing on a different aspect of risk assessment. Following this introduction, Chapter 2 covers the identification and analysis of risks. Chapter 3 focuses on risk mitigation and management. Chapter 4 covers uncertainty and its role in risk assessment. Chapters 5 to 9 focus on specific areas of risk assessment, including financial, operational, health and safety, environmental, and legal and compliance risks. Finally, Chapter 10 provides a conclusion and outlook for the future of risk assessment.

CHAPTER 2

IDENTIFYING AND ANALYZING RISKS

2.1 INTRODUCTION

The identification and analysis of risks is the first step in the risk assessment process. The objective of this chapter is to provide a comprehensive overview of best practices for identifying and analyzing risks, including the use of various tools and techniques.

2.2 RISK IDENTIFICATION

Risk identification is the process of identifying and documenting potential risks that could impact an organization or project. There are several methods for identifying risks, including:

- Brainstorming: Involves a group of people discussing potential risks and recording their ideas.

- SWOT analysis: A structured approach to analyzing the internal and external factors that could impact an organization or project.

- Scenario analysis: Involves considering potential scenarios and the risks associated with each.

2.3 RISK ANALYSIS

Once risks have been identified, they must be analyzed to determine their likelihood and potential impact. There are several methods for analyzing risks, including:

- **Probabilistic analysis:** Involves quantifying the likelihood of a risk occurring, often by calculating the probability of an event.

- **Impact analysis:** Involves assessing the potential consequences of a risk occurring, such as loss of revenue, damage to reputation, or harm to people.

- **Likelihood-impact analysis**: Involves combining the results of the probabilistic and impact analyses to assess the overall risk.

2.4 BEST PRACTICES FOR IDENTIFYING AND ANALYZING RISKS

The following are best practices for identifying and analyzing risks:

- **Collaboration:** Involve key stakeholders in the risk identification and analysis process to ensure that all risks are considered.

- **Thoroughness:** Ensure that all potential risks are identified and analyzed, including both known and unknown risks.

- **Documentation:** Document the results of the risk identification and analysis process to ensure that risks are consistently understood and managed.

- **Regular review:** Regularly review and update the risk identification and analysis process to ensure that risks are effectively managed.

2.5 CONCLUSION

In conclusion, the identification and analysis of risks is a critical component of the risk assessment process. By using best practices for risk identification and analysis, organizations can ensure that they are effectively prepared to manage risks, improve decision-making, and allocate resources more effectively.

CHAPTER 3

RISK MITIGATION AND MANAGEMENT

3.1 INTRODUCTION

Once risks have been identified and analyzed, the next step is to develop and implement strategies to mitigate or manage those risks. The objective of this chapter is to provide an overview of best practices for risk mitigation and management.

3.2 RISK MITIGATION

Risk mitigation is the process of reducing the likelihood or impact of a risk. The following are common strategies for mitigating risks:

- **Avoidance:** Refers to avoiding the risk altogether by not pursuing an activity or project that would expose the organization to the risk.

- **Transfer:** Involves transferring the risk to another party, such as through insurance or a contract.

- **Reduction:** Involves reducing the likelihood or impact of a risk, such as by implementing risk-management controls or improving processes.

3.3 RISK MANAGEMENT

Risk management is the process of identifying, analyzing, and mitigating risks. The following are best practices for risk management:

- **Integration:** Integrate risk management into all aspects of the organization's decision-making process to ensure that risks are consistently considered.

- **Communication:** Ensure that key stakeholders are informed of risks and the strategies in place to manage those risks.

- **Monitoring:** Regularly monitor risks and the effectiveness of risk-management strategies to ensure that risks are effectively managed.

- **Review and adjustment:** Regularly review and adjust risk-management strategies to ensure that they remain effective in light of changes in the risk landscape.

3.4 RISK-MANAGEMENT CONTROLS

Risk-management controls are mechanisms or strategies that are put in place to mitigate or manage risks. The following are common types of risk-management controls:

- **Technical controls:** Involve the use of technology to mitigate risks, such as firewalls or encryption.

- **Administrative controls:** Involve the use of policies and procedures to mitigate risks, such as security awareness training or background checks.

- **Physical controls:** Involve the use of physical barriers or access controls to mitigate risks, such as security cameras or access cards.

3.5 CONCLUSION

In conclusion, risk mitigation and management is a critical component of the risk assessment process. By following best practices for risk mitigation and management and implementing effective risk-management controls, organizations can improve their ability to manage risks, minimize their exposure to risks, and allocate resources more effectively.

CHAPTER 4

UNDERSTANDING AND EVALUATING UNCERTAINTY

4.1 INTRODUCTION

Uncertainty is a central concept in risk assessment and management, as it refers to the lack of certainty about future events and their potential impact. The objective of this chapter is to provide an overview of best practices for understanding and evaluating uncertainty.

4.2 TYPES OF UNCERTAINTY

Uncertainty can be categorized into two main types:

- Aleatory uncertainty: Refers to inherent variability in events, such as the unpredictability of natural disasters or market fluctuations.

- Epistemic uncertainty: Refers to uncertainty about the knowledge of a system or event, such as limited data or a lack of understanding of a process.

4.3 EVALUATING UNCERTAINTY

Evaluating uncertainty involves quantifying the level of uncertainty associated with a particular event or outcome. There are several methods for evaluating uncertainty, including:

- **Sensitivity analysis:** Involves analyzing the impact of changes in variables on the outcome of a risk analysis.

- **Scenario analysis:** Involves considering potential scenarios and the risks associated with each.

- **Monte Carlo simulation:** Involves modeling the interactions of variables and generating a range of potential outcomes.

4.4 BEST PRACTICES FOR EVALUATING UNCERTAINTY

The following are best practices for evaluating uncertainty:

- Consider multiple sources of uncertainty: Consider both aleatory and epistemic uncertainty in your analysis.

- Quantify uncertainty: Use methods such as sensitivity analysis, scenario analysis, and Monte Carlo simulation to quantify uncertainty.

- Communicate uncertainty: Clearly communicate the level of uncertainty associated with risks to key stakeholders, including the potential impact of uncertainty on decision-making.

- Regular review: Regularly review and update the evaluation of uncertainty to ensure that it remains accurate and relevant.

 SkillWeed

4.5 CONCLUSION

In conclusion, understanding and evaluating uncertainty is a critical component of the risk assessment process. By following best practices for evaluating uncertainty, organizations can improve their ability to make informed decisions and allocate resources more effectively in light of uncertain future events.

CHAPTER 5

FINANCIAL RISK ASSESSMENT

5.1 INTRODUCTION

Financial risk is the risk of loss associated with financial instruments or investments. The objective of this chapter is to provide an overview of best practices for financial risk assessment.

5.2 TYPES OF FINANCIAL RISK

Financial risk can be categorized into several types, including:

- **Market risk:** Refers to the risk of loss associated with changes in the value of a financial instrument or investment, such as stock price fluctuations.

- **Credit risk:** Refers to the risk of loss associated with the default or bankruptcy of a borrower, such as a company or individual.

- **Liquidity risk:** Refers to the risk of loss associated with an inability to access funds in a timely manner, such as in the case of a sudden market downturn.

- **Operational risk:** Refers to the risk of loss associated with operational failure, such as fraud, system failure, or human error.

5.3 EVALUATING FINANCIAL RISK

Evaluating financial risk involves quantifying the level of risk associated with financial instruments or investments. There are several methods for evaluating financial risk, including:

- **Value at Risk (VaR):** A statistical measure that quantifies the level of risk associated with an investment.

- **Stress testing:** Involves simulating adverse scenarios and their potential impact on financial instruments or investments.

- **Portfolio analysis:** Involves analyzing the risk and return of a portfolio of investments.

5.4 BEST PRACTICES FOR FINANCIAL RISK ASSESSMENT

The following are best practices for financial risk assessment:

- **Consider multiple sources of financial risk:** Consider market risk, credit risk, liquidity risk, and operational risk in your analysis.

- **Quantify financial risk:** Use methods such as VaR, stress testing, and portfolio analysis to quantify financial risk.

- **Regular review:** Regularly review and update the assessment of financial risk to ensure that it remains accurate and relevant.

- **Integration:** Integrate financial risk assessment into all aspects of the organization's decision-making process to ensure that risks are consistently considered.

5.5 CONCLUSION

In conclusion, financial risk assessment is a critical component of the risk assessment process, particularly for organizations with significant exposure to financial instruments or investments. By following best practices for financial risk assessment, organizations can improve their ability to make informed decisions and allocate resources more effectively in light of potential financial risks.

CHAPTER 6

OPERATIONAL RISK ASSESSMENT

6.1 INTRODUCTION

Operational risk refers to the risk of loss associated with the failure of internal processes, systems, human error, or external events. The objective of this chapter is to provide an overview of best practices for operational risk assessment.

6.2 IDENTIFYING OPERATIONAL RISKS

Operational risks can be identified through a variety of methods, including:

- **Root cause analysis:** Involves analyzing the underlying causes of operational failures to identify potential risks.

- **Internal audits:** Involves reviewing internal processes and systems to identify potential risks.

- **External assessments:** Involves engaging external experts to assess the organization's exposure to operational risks.

6.3 EVALUATING OPERATIONAL RISK

Evaluating operational risk involves quantifying the level of risk associated with potential operational failures. There are several methods for evaluating operational risk, including:

- Loss event frequency: Involves analyzing the frequency of past operational failures to identify potential risks.

- Impact analysis: Involves quantifying the potential impact of operational failures on the organization.

- Key risk indicators: Involves monitoring key performance indicators to identify potential operational risks.

6.4 BEST PRACTICES FOR OPERATIONAL RISK ASSESSMENT

The following are best practices for operational risk assessment:

- Consider multiple sources of operational risk: Consider internal processes, systems, human error, and external events in your analysis.

- Quantify operational risk: Use methods such as loss event frequency, impact analysis, and key risk indicators to quantify operational risk.

- Regular review: Regularly review and update the assessment of operational risk to ensure that it remains accurate and relevant.

- Integration: Integrate operational risk assessment into all aspects of the organization's decision-making process to ensure that risks are consistently considered.

6.5 CONCLUSION

In conclusion, operational risk assessment is a critical component of the risk assessment process, particularly for organizations with complex operations. By following best practices for operational risk assessment, organizations can improve their ability to make informed decisions and allocate resources more effectively in light of potential operational risks.

CHAPTER 7

HEALTH AND SAFETY RISK ASSESSMENT

7.1 INTRODUCTION

Health and safety risks refer to the risk of harm to individuals as a result of work activities or the environment. The objective of this chapter is to provide an overview of best practices for health and safety risk assessment.

7.2 IDENTIFYING HEALTH AND SAFETY RISKS

Health and safety risks can be identified through a variety of methods, including:

- Worksite inspections: Involves physically inspecting the worksite to identify potential health and safety risks.

- Employee interviews: Involves speaking with employees to identify potential health and safety risks from their perspective.

- Industry standards: Involves reviewing industry standards to identify potential health and safety risks.

7.3 EVALUATING HEALTH AND SAFETY RISK

Evaluating health and safety risk involves quantifying the level of risk associated with potential harm to individuals. There are several methods for evaluating health and safety risk, including:

- Hazard identification: Involves identifying potential sources of harm, such as machinery or hazardous substances.

- Risk assessment matrix: Involves ranking the likelihood and potential impact of potential hazards to determine the level of risk.

- Risk control hierarchy: Involves prioritizing risk mitigation measures based on the level of risk, such as elimination, substitution, engineering controls, administrative controls, and personal protective equipment.

7.4 BEST PRACTICES FOR HEALTH AND SAFETY RISK ASSESSMENT

The following are best practices for health and safety risk assessment:

- Consider multiple sources of health and safety risk: Consider worksite inspections, employee interviews, and industry standards in your analysis.

- Quantify health and safety risk: Use methods such as hazard identification, risk assessment matrix, and risk control hierarchy to quantify health and safety risk.

- Regular review: Regularly review and update the assessment of health and safety risk to ensure that it remains accurate and relevant.

- Integration: Integrate health and safety risk assessment into all aspects of the organization's decision-making process to ensure that risks are consistently considered.

7.5 CONCLUSION

In conclusion, health and safety risk assessment is a critical component of the risk assessment process, particularly for organizations with responsibility for employee health and safety. By following best practices for health and safety risk assessment, organizations can improve their ability to make informed decisions and allocate resources more effectively in light of potential health and safety risks.

CHAPTER 8
ENVIRONMENTAL RISK ASSESSMENT

8.1 INTRODUCTION

Environmental risks refer to the potential harm to the environment as a result of work activities or the surrounding environment. The objective of this chapter is to provide an overview of best practices for environmental risk assessment.

8.2 IDENTIFYING ENVIRONMENTAL RISKS

Environmental risks can be identified through a variety of methods, including:

- Worksite inspections: Involves physically inspecting the worksite to identify potential environmental risks.

- Industry standards: Involves reviewing industry standards to identify potential environmental risks.

- Stakeholder consultation: Involves consulting with stakeholders, such as local communities, to identify potential environmental risks.

8.3 EVALUATING ENVIRONMENTAL RISK

Evaluating environmental risk involves quantifying the level of risk associated with potential harm to the environment. There are several methods for evaluating environmental risk, including:

- Hazard identification: Involves identifying potential sources of harm to the environment, such as air pollution or water pollution.

- Risk assessment matrix: Involves ranking the likelihood and potential impact of potential hazards to determine the level of risk.

- Risk control hierarchy: Involves prioritizing risk mitigation measures based on the level of risk, such as elimination, substitution, engineering controls, administrative controls, and personal protective equipment.

8.4 BEST PRACTICES FOR ENVIRONMENTAL RISK ASSESSMENT

The following are best practices for environmental risk assessment:

- Consider multiple sources of environmental risk: Consider worksite inspections, industry standards, and stakeholder consultation in your analysis.

- Quantify environmental risk: Use methods such as hazard identification, risk assessment matrix, and risk control hierarchy to quantify environmental risk.

- Regular review: Regularly review and update the assessment of environmental risk to ensure that it remains accurate and relevant.

- Integration: Integrate environmental risk assessment into all aspects of the organization's decision-making process to ensure that risks are consistently considered.

8.5 CONCLUSION

In conclusion, environmental risk assessment is a critical component of the risk assessment process, particularly for organizations with responsibility for the environment. By following best practices for environmental risk assessment, organizations can improve their ability to make informed decisions and allocate resources more effectively in light of potential environmental risks.

CHAPTER 9

LEGAL AND COMPLIANCE RISK ASSESSMENT

9.1 INTRODUCTION

L egal and compliance risks refer to the potential exposure to legal penalties or regulatory sanctions as a result of non-compliance with laws and regulations. The objective of this chapter is to provide an overview of best practices for legal and compliance risk assessment.

9.2 IDENTIFYING LEGAL AND COMPLIANCE RISKS

Legal and compliance risks can be identified through a variety of methods, including:

- **Legal research:** Involves reviewing relevant laws and regulations to identify potential compliance risks.

- **Stakeholder consultation:** Involves consulting with stakeholders, such as legal experts and industry associations, to identify potential legal and compliance risks.

- **Internal audits:** Involves reviewing internal policies and procedures to identify potential compliance risks.

9.3 EVALUATING LEGAL AND COMPLIANCE RISK

Evaluating legal and compliance risk involves quantifying the level of risk associated with non-compliance with laws and regulations. There are several methods for evaluating legal and compliance risk, including:

- **Risk assessment matrix:** Involves ranking the likelihood and potential impact of potential non-compliance to determine the level of risk.

- **Compliance audit:** Involves reviewing the organization's policies and procedures to determine the level of compliance with laws and regulations.

- **Legal liability assessment:** Involves evaluating the potential legal exposure of the organization in the event of non-compliance.

9.4 BEST PRACTICES FOR LEGAL AND COMPLIANCE RISK ASSESSMENT

The following are best practices for legal and compliance risk assessment:

- **Consider multiple sources of legal and compliance risk:** Consider legal research, stakeholder consultation, and internal audits in your analysis.

- **Quantify legal and compliance risk:** Use methods such as risk assessment matrix, compliance audit, and legal liability assessment to quantify legal and compliance risk.

- **Regular review:** Regularly review and update the assessment of legal and compliance risk to ensure that it remains accurate and relevant.

- **Integration:** Integrate legal and compliance risk assessment into all aspects of the organization's decision-making process to ensure that risks are consistently considered.

9.5 CONCLUSION

In conclusion, legal and compliance risk assessment is a critical component of the risk assessment process, particularly for organizations with legal and regulatory obligations. By following best practices for legal and compliance risk assessment, organizations can improve their ability to make informed decisions and allocate resources more effectively in light of potential legal and compliance risks.

CHAPTER 10

CONCLUSION AND FUTURE DIRECTIONS

10.1 OVERVIEW

The objective of this chapter is to provide a summary of the key concepts and best practices discussed in the book and to outline potential future directions for risk assessment.

10.2 KEY CONCEPTS AND BEST PRACTICES

In the previous chapters, we discussed the following key concepts and best practices for risk assessment:

The importance of understanding the risk environment and the role of risk assessment in decision making.

- The process of identifying and analyzing risks, including the use of different methods such as scenario analysis and SWOT analysis.

- The importance of considering multiple sources of risk and considering both qualitative and quantitative data in risk assessment.

- The process of risk mitigation and management, including the use of mitigation strategies such as risk transfer and risk reduction.

- The evaluation of uncertainty and the importance of considering the level of certainty in risk assessments.

- The assessment of financial, operational, health and safety, environmental, and legal and compliance risks.

10.3 FUTURE DIRECTIONS FOR RISK ASSESSMENT

The field of risk assessment is constantly evolving, and there are several potential future directions for risk assessment, including:

- Integration of artificial intelligence and machine learning: The increasing use of artificial intelligence and machine learning in risk assessment can help organizations to identify and analyze risks more effectively and to make more informed decisions.

- Greater focus on stakeholder engagement: There is a growing recognition of the importance of stakeholder engagement in risk assessment, and organizations are increasingly seeking to involve stakeholders in the risk assessment process.

- Increased use of scenario analysis: Scenario analysis is becoming increasingly popular as a tool for risk assessment, as it allows organizations to consider multiple potential futures and to make more informed decisions in light of uncertainty.

- Greater focus on sustainability: There is a growing recognition of the importance of sustainability in risk assessment, and organizations are increasingly considering the long-term impacts of their activities on the environment and society.

10.4 CONCLUSION

In conclusion, risk assessment is a critical component of decision making, and by following best practices for risk assessment, organizations can improve their ability to make informed decisions and to allocate resources more effectively in light of potential risks. The field of risk assessment is constantly evolving, and there are several potential future directions for risk assessment, including the integration of artificial intelligence and machine learning, increased focus on stakeholder engagement, increased use of scenario analysis, and greater focus on sustainability.

RISK MANAGEMENT FRAMEWORK (RMF)

Risk Management Framework (RMF) is a structured approach to managing risks that provides a set of guidelines and procedures for identifying, assessing, prioritizing, and managing risks to an organization's operations, assets, and individuals. RMF is often used in the context of cybersecurity and information technology, but it can be applied to any area where risks need to be managed.

THE RMF PROCESS INVOLVES SIX STEPS:

Categorize Information Systems: The first step is to identify and categorize the information systems and data that need to be protected based on their mission, business processes, and the types of information they contain.

Select Security Controls: The second step is to select a set of security controls that are appropriate for the categorized information systems based on the risks and the organization's risk tolerance.

Implement Security Controls: The third step is to implement the selected security controls in a systematic and consistent manner to ensure that they function as intended and meet the organization's security requirements.

Assess Security Controls: The fourth step is to assess the effectiveness of the implemented security controls and determine whether they are operating as intended and meeting the organization's security requirements.

Authorize Information Systems: The fifth step is to authorize the information systems for operation based on the risk assessment and security control assessment results.

Monitor Security Controls: The final step is to continuously monitor and assess the security controls to ensure that they are functioning as intended and meeting the organization's security requirements.

The RMF process is iterative and ongoing, with each step influencing the others. It provides a comprehensive and structured approach to managing risks that can help organizations to identify, assess, and mitigate risks to their operations, assets, and individuals.

Risk management is the process of identifying, assessing, and mitigating risks to an organization. A risk management framework is a structured approach to managing risks that provides a set of guidelines and procedures for identifying, assessing, prioritizing, and managing risks. Here are the steps involved in a risk management framework, along with examples and best practices:

ESTABLISH CONTEXT:

The first step is to establish the context in which the risk management framework will operate. This involves identifying the organization's objectives, stakeholders, and risk appetite.

- **Example:** A manufacturing company's objective is to produce high-quality products while minimizing production costs. Its stakeholders include customers, employees, shareholders, and suppliers. The company's risk appetite is to take calculated risks to achieve its objectives.

- **Best Practice:** The organization should define the scope of the risk management framework and ensure that it aligns with its overall strategy and objectives.

RISK IDENTIFICATION:

The second step is to identify the risks that the organization may face. This involves identifying potential risks and events that could impact the organization's objectives.

- **Example:** The manufacturing company's risks could include supply chain disruptions, product defects, workplace accidents, and regulatory compliance issues.

- **Best Practice:** The organization should involve all relevant stakeholders in the risk identification process and use various tools and techniques such as risk assessments, audits, and interviews.

RISK ASSESSMENT:

The third step is to assess the likelihood and impact of each identified risk. This involves analyzing the probability and severity of each risk.

- **Example:** The manufacturing company might assess the likelihood and impact of a supply chain disruption by analyzing its supplier's financial stability and production capacity.

- **Best Practice:** The organization should use standardized criteria to assess and prioritize risks, and use quantitative and qualitative data to support risk assessments.

RISK MITIGATION:

The fourth step is to develop and implement strategies to mitigate the risks. This involves identifying and evaluating possible risk treatment options and selecting the most effective strategy.

- **Example:** The manufacturing company might mitigate the risk of supply chain disruptions by diversifying its suppliers, implementing inventory management systems, or establishing backup production facilities.

- **Best Practice:** The organization should involve relevant stakeholders in the risk mitigation process and regularly review and update risk treatment strategies.

RISK MONITORING AND REVIEW:

The fifth and final step is to monitor and review the effectiveness of the risk management framework. This involves regularly monitoring and reviewing the risk management processes and outcomes to ensure that they are aligned with the organization's objectives.

- **Example:** The manufacturing company might regularly monitor its suppliers' financial stability and production capacity to ensure continuity of supply.

- **Best Practice:** The organization should establish a system for ongoing monitoring and review of risks and risk management activities, and regularly report on the effectiveness of the risk management framework to senior management and relevant stakeholders.

In summary, a risk management framework involves establishing context, identifying risks, assessing risks, mitigating risks, and monitoring and reviewing the effectiveness of the risk management processes. Best practices for risk management include involving relevant stakeholders, using standardized criteria and data, regularly reviewing and updating risk treatment strategies, and establishing a system for ongoing monitoring and review of risks.

INTERVIEW SCENARIOS

The interview questions and answers are designed for the role of an IT Risk Analyst, and they follow the STAR model, which stands for Situation, Task, Action, and Result. This model is used to structure responses to interview questions in a way that is easy to understand and provides a clear example of how the candidate has dealt with similar situations in the past.

Situation	Task	Action	Result
A new employee is hired and given access to the company's network	Assess the risk of unauthorized access to sensitive data	Conduct a review of the employee's access permissions and monitor their activity	Reduce the risk of data breaches and unauthorized access
A software upgrade is planned for critical business systems	Assess the risk of system downtime and data loss	Conduct a risk analysis of the upgrade process and create a backup plan	Minimize the risk of system downtime and data loss during the upgrade
A company laptop is stolen from an employee's car	Assess the risk of data theft and privacy breaches	Activate remote wipe and tracking capabilities on the laptop	Prevent data theft and unauthorized access to company data
A new software vendor is being considered for a business critical system	Assess the risk of vendor selection and integration	Conduct a vendor risk assessment and evaluate their software integration capabilities	Reduce the risk of software integration issues and vendor performance issues
A phishing email is received by multiple employees	Assess the risk of a security breach and data loss	Conduct a security audit of affected systems and educate employees on phishing awareness	Minimize the risk of security breaches and data loss due to phishing attacks
A server room is experiencing environmental control issues	Assess the risk of hardware failure and data loss	Conduct a review of the server room environment and	Ensure hardware reliability and minimize the risk of data loss

Situation	Task	Action	Result
		implement necessary changes	
An employee's account is compromised and used to access company data	Assess the risk of unauthorized access and data breaches	Investigate the extent of the breach and implement additional security measures	Minimize the risk of data breaches and unauthorized access
A new third-party software is being considered for use	Assess the risk of software compatibility and security vulnerabilities	Conduct a software risk assessment and evaluate the vendor's security protocols	Reduce the risk of software compatibility issues and security vulnerabilities
A natural disaster damages a company's data center	Assess the risk of data loss and system downtime	Activate disaster recovery procedures and migrate data to backup systems	Minimize the risk of data loss and system downtime
A security breach occurs due to a weak password policy	Assess the risk of data loss and unauthorized access	Implement a new password policy and educate employees on password security	Minimize the risk of security breaches and unauthorized access due to weak passwords